TAKE NOTE!

TO ACCOMPANY

PSYCHOLOGY IN ACTION

Fifth Edition

Karen Huffman
Palomar College

Mark Vernoy
Palomar College

Judith Vernoy

JOHN WILEY & SONS, INC.
New York • Chichester • Weinheim
Brisbane • Singapore • Toronto

To order books or for customer service call 1-800-CALL-WILEY (225-5945).

ISBN 0-471-35957-2

Printed in the United States of America

10 9 8 7 6 5 4 3 2 1

Printed and bound by Courier Westford, Inc.

HOW TO USE TAKE NOTE

This easy-to-carry paperback contains many of the illustrations found in your text. When your instructor discusses one of these figures in class, you can annotate the illustration right in this book. This frees you up to concentrate on the lecture rather than having to quickly recreate an illustration in order to annotate it. It also makes it easy to organize your notes for study later on.

The illustrations you'll find in these pages are exact replicas of the illustrations in your textbook. Some images may be slightly fuzzy or may not reflect the true colors of the originals. We chose not to duplicate the quality and color in the textbook so that we could minimize the cost to you. When you use this reasonably-priced notebook alongside your textbook, you've got a powerful organizational and study tool!

CONTENTS

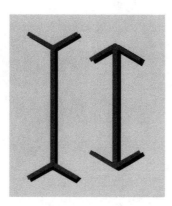

1

FIGURE 1.1

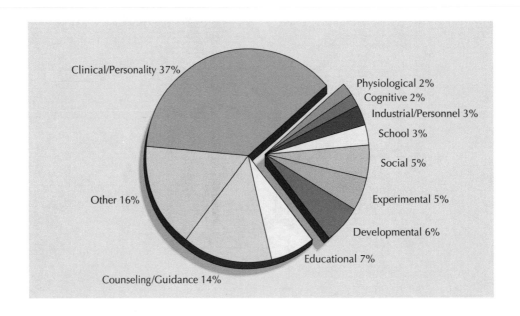

Clinical/Personality 37%

Physiological 2%
Cognitive 2%
Industrial/Personnel 3%
School 3%
Social 5%
Experimental 5%
Developmental 6%
Educational 7%

Other 16%

Counseling/Guidance 14%

FIGURE 1.2

2

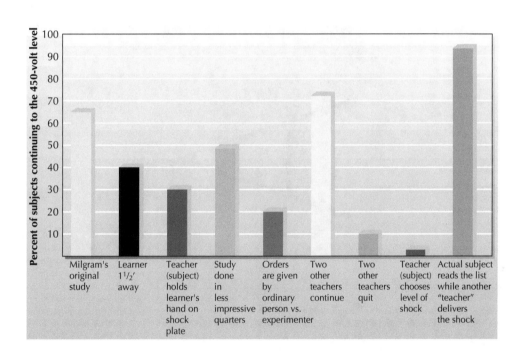

FIGURE 1.3

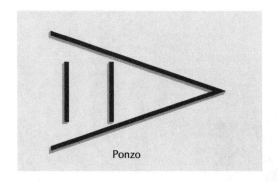

Ponzo

FIGURE 1.4

	Sunday	Monday	Tuesday	Wednesday	Thursday	Friday	Saturday
7:00		Breakfast		Breakfast		Breakfast	
8:00		History	Breakfast	History	Breakfast	History	
9:00		Psychology	Statistics	Psychology	Statistics	Psychology	
10:00		Review History & Psychology	Campus Job	Review History & Psychology	Statistics Lab	Review History & Psychology	
11:00		Biology		Biology		Biology	
12:00		Lunch / Study		Exercise	Lunch	Exercise	
1:00		Bio Lab	Lunch	Lunch	Study	Lunch	
2:00			Study	Study			

5

FIGURE 1.5

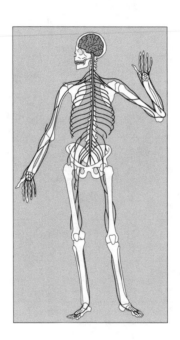

FIGURE 2.1   6

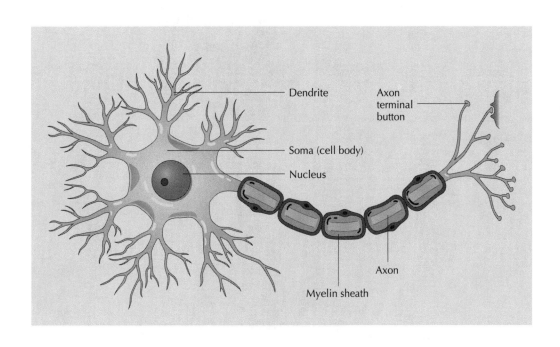

Dendrite

Soma (cell body)

Nucleus

Axon
terminal
button

Axon

Myelin sheath

FIGURE 2.2

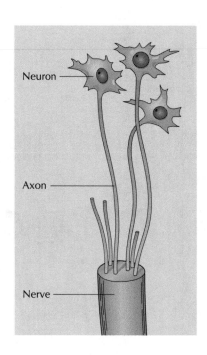

FIGURE 2.3 8

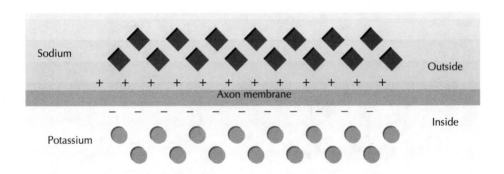

Sodium

Outside

Axon membrane

Inside

Potassium

FIGURE 2.4

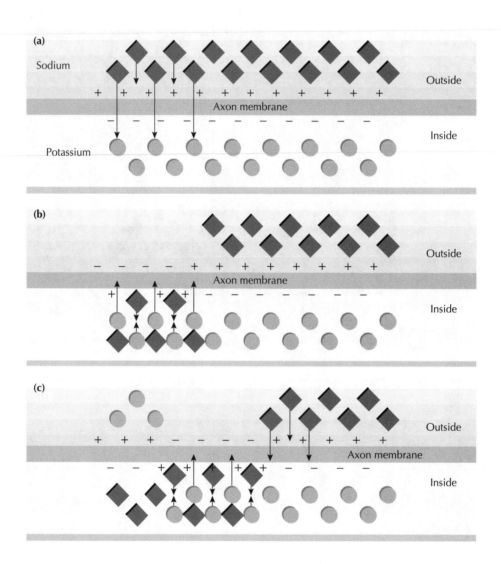

(a)

Sodium

Outside

Axon membrane

Inside

Potassium

(b)

Outside

Axon membrane

Inside

(c)

Outside

Axon membrane

Inside

FIGURE 2.5

10

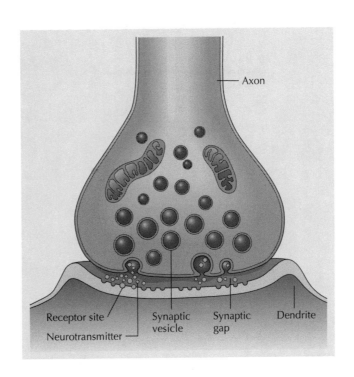

Axon

Receptor site

Neurotransmitter

Synaptic vesicle

Synaptic gap

Dendrite

11

FIGURE 2.6

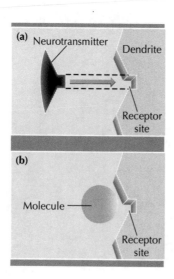

(a) Neurotransmitter   Dendrite

Receptor site

(b) Molecule

Receptor site

FIGURE 2.7   12

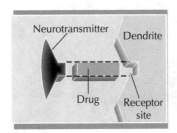

FIGURE 2.8

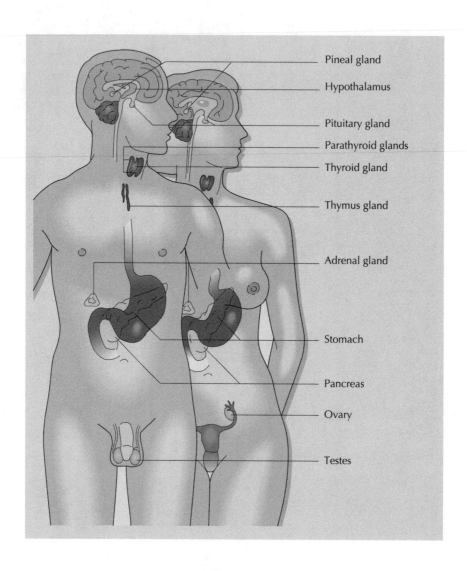

Pineal gland

Hypothalamus

Pituitary gland

Parathyroid glands

Thyroid gland

Thymus gland

Adrenal gland

Stomach

Pancreas

Ovary

Testes

FIGURE 2.9

14

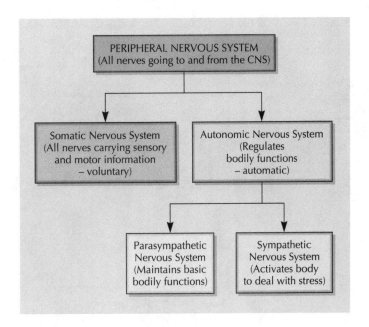

FIGURE 2.10

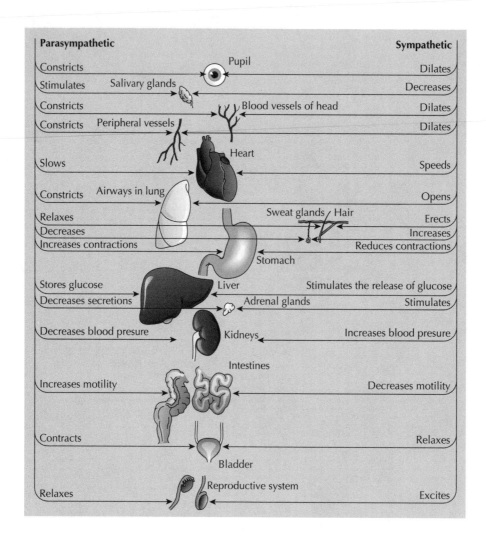

Parasympathetic   **Sympathetic**

Constricts — Pupil — Dilates

Stimulates — Salivary glands — Decreases

Constricts — Blood vessels of head — Dilates

Constricts — Peripheral vessels — Dilates

Slows — Heart — Speeds

Constricts — Airways in lung — Opens

Relaxes — Sweat glands / Hair — Erects

Decreases — Increases

Increases contractions — Stomach — Reduces contractions

Stores glucose — Liver — Stimulates the release of glucose

Decreases secretions — Adrenal glands — Stimulates

Decreases blood presure — Kidneys — Increases blood presure

Intestines

Increases motility — Decreases motility

Contracts — Bladder — Relaxes

Relaxes — Reproductive system — Excites

FIGURE 2.11   16

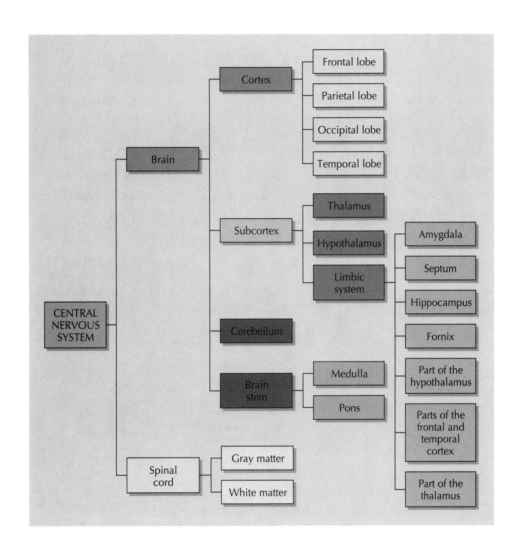

FIGURE 2.12

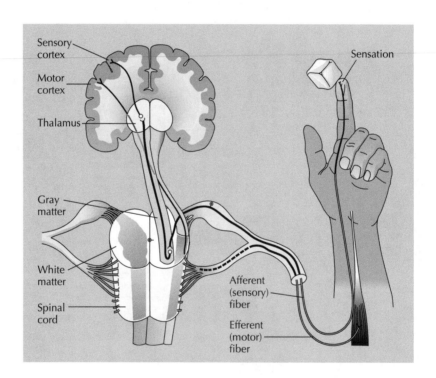

Sensory cortex

Motor cortex

Thalamus

Gray matter

White matter

Spinal cord

Sensation

Afferent (sensory) fiber

Efferent (motor) fiber

FIGURE 2.13

18

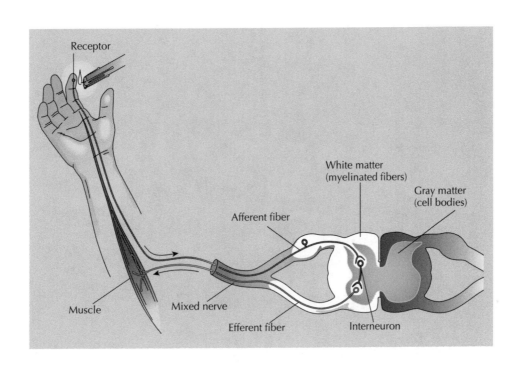

Receptor

White matter
(myelinated fibers)

Gray matter
(cell bodies)

Afferent fiber

Muscle

Mixed nerve

Efferent fiber

Interneuron

FIGURE 2.14

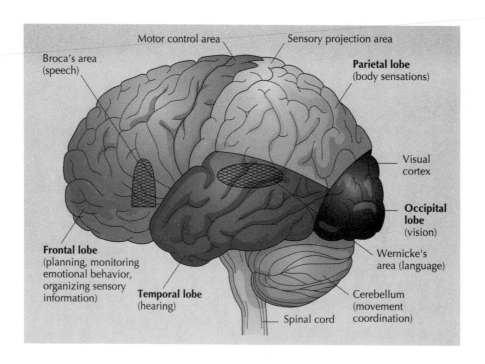

Motor control area

Sensory projection area

Broca's area
(speech)

Parietal lobe
(body sensations)

Visual
cortex

**Occipital
lobe**
(vision)

Frontal lobe
(planning, monitoring
emotional behavior,
organizing sensory
information)

Wernicke's
area (language)

Temporal lobe
(hearing)

Cerebellum
(movement
coordination)

Spinal cord

FIGURE 2.15

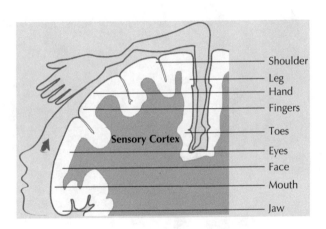

Shoulder
Leg
Hand
Fingers
Toes
Eyes
Face
Mouth
Jaw

Sensory Cortex

FIGURE 2.16

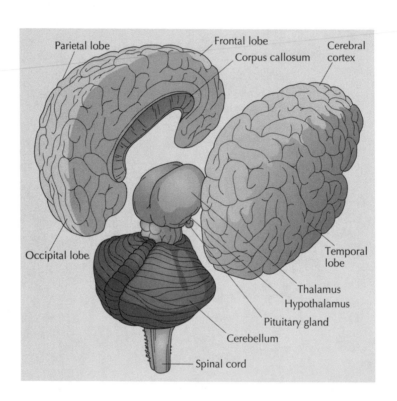

FIGURE 2.17

22

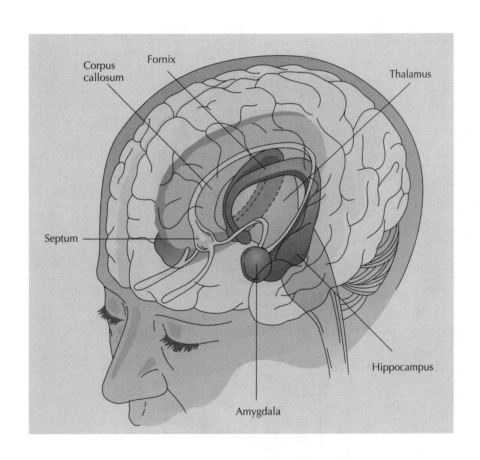

FIGURE 2.18

Problem-Solving Tasks Favoring Women

Perceptual speed:
As quickly as possible identify matching items.

Displaced objects:
After looking at the middle picture, tell which item is missing from the the picture on the right.

Verbal fluency:
List words that begin with the same letter. (Women also tend to perform better in ideational fluency tests, for example, listing objects that are the same color.)

B – – –	Bat, big, bike, bang, bark, bank, bring, brand, broom, bright, brook bug, buddy, bunk

Precision manual tasks:
Place the pegs in the holes as quickly as possible.

Mathematical calculation:
Compute the answer.

72	$6(18+4)-78+\frac{36}{2}$

FIGURE 2.20

24

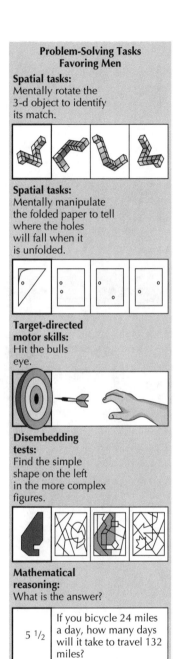

Problem-Solving Tasks Favoring Men

Spatial tasks:
Mentally rotate the 3-d object to identify its match.

Spatial tasks:
Mentally manipulate the folded paper to tell where the holes will fall when it is unfolded.

Target-directed motor skills:
Hit the bulls eye.

Disembedding tests:
Find the simple shape on the left in the more complex figures.

Mathematical reasoning:
What is the answer?

| 5 1/2 | If you bicycle 24 miles a day, how many days will it take to travel 132 miles? |

FIGURE 2.21

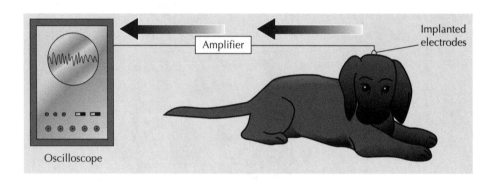

Oscilloscope

Amplifier

Implanted electrodes

FIGURE 2.23

26

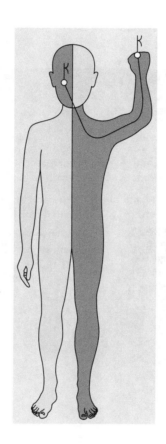

FIGURE 2.24

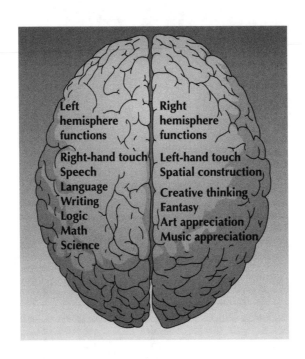

FIGURE 2.25

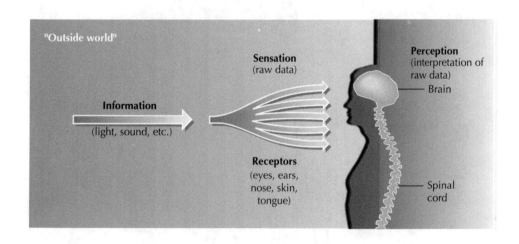

FIGURE 3.1

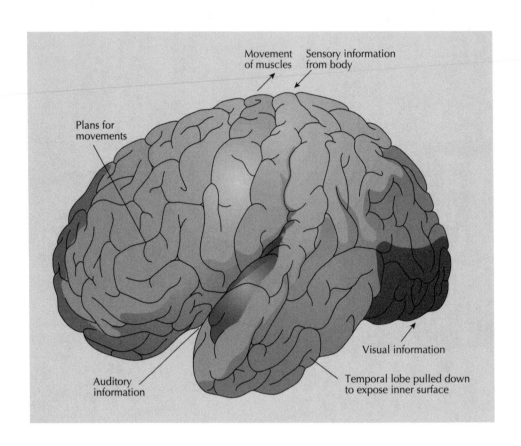

FIGURE 3.2   30

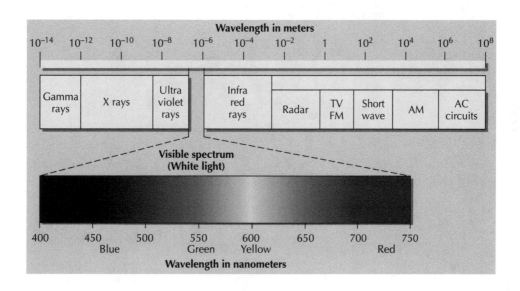

FIGURE 3.3

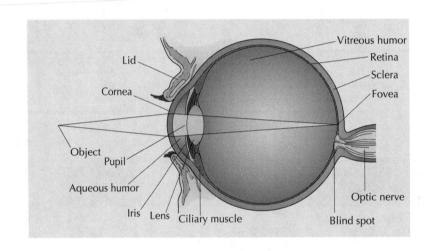

FIGURE 3.4   32

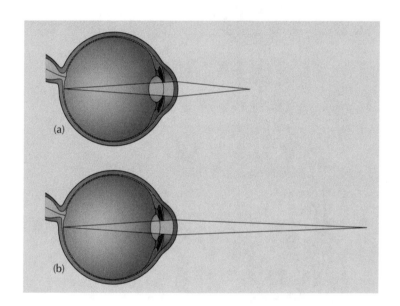

(a)

(b)

FIGURE 3.5

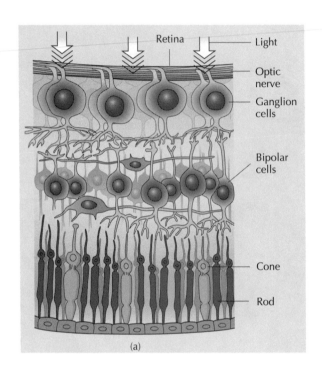

(a)

FIGURE 3.6a 34

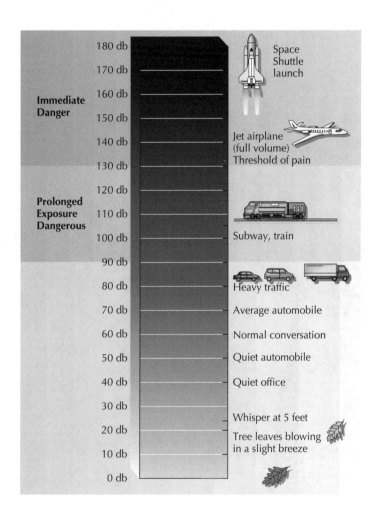

FIGURE 3.7

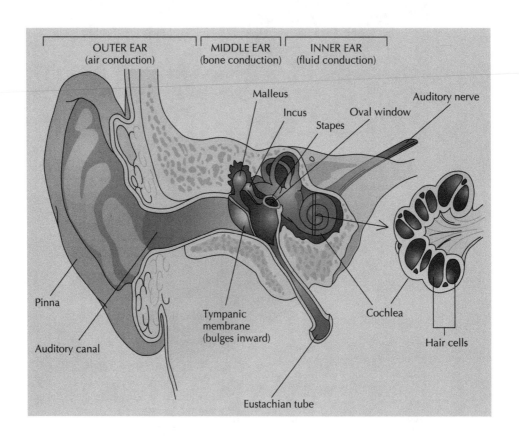

OUTER EAR
(air conduction)

MIDDLE EAR
(bone conduction)

INNER EAR
(fluid conduction)

Malleus

Incus

Stapes

Oval window

Auditory nerve

Pinna

Auditory canal

Tympanic
membrane
(bulges inward)

Cochlea

Hair cells

Eustachian tube

FIGURE 3.8

36

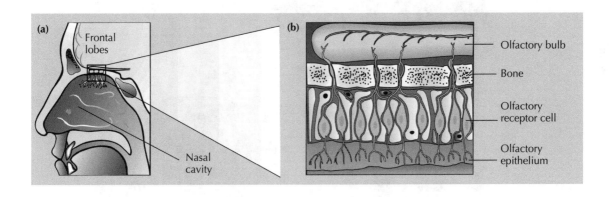

FIGURE 3.9

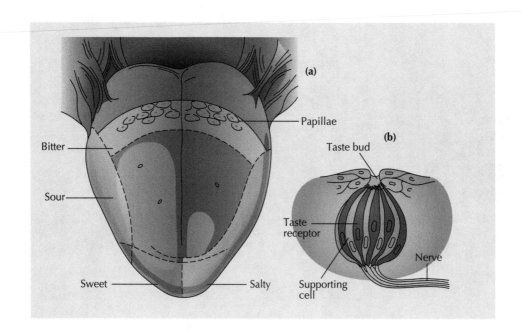

(a)

Papillae

(b)

Taste bud

Bitter

Sour

Taste
receptor

Nerve

Sweet

Salty

Supporting
cell

FIGURE 3.10   38

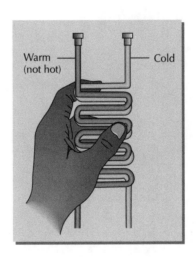

FIGURE 3.11

FIGURE 3.13   40

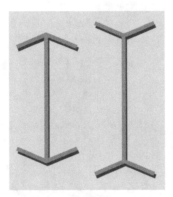

FIGURE 3.14

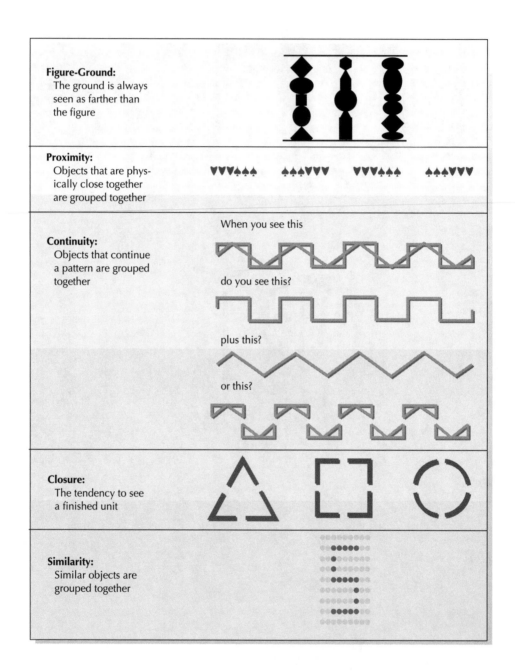

Figure-Ground:
The ground is always seen as farther than the figure

Proximity:
Objects that are physically close together are grouped together

Continuity:
Objects that continue a pattern are grouped together

When you see this

do you see this?

plus this?

or this?

Closure:
The tendency to see a finished unit

Similarity:
Similar objects are grouped together

FIGURE 3.15

42

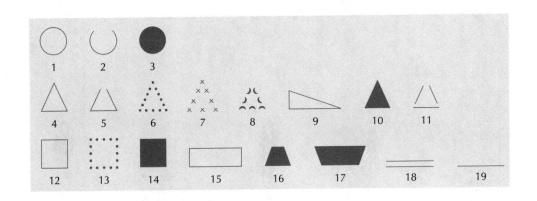

FIGURE 3.16

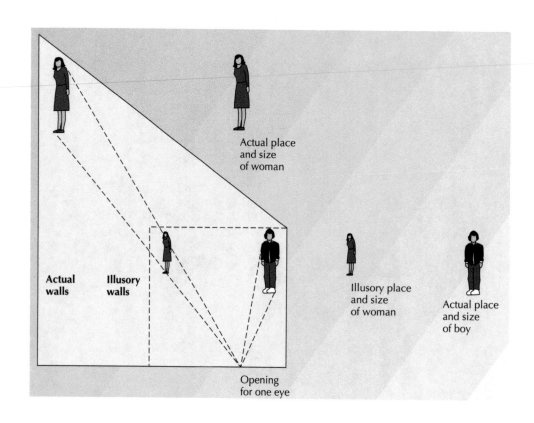

Actual place
and size
of woman

Actual
walls

Illusory
walls

Illusory place
and size
of woman

Actual place
and size
of boy

Opening
for one eye

FIGURE 3.17   44

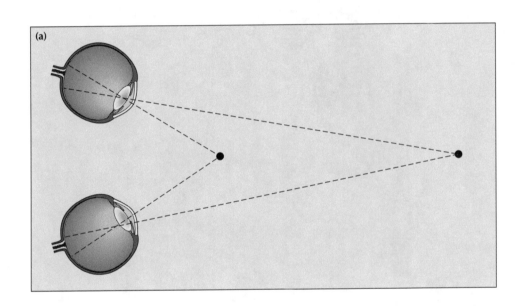

FIGURE 3.18a

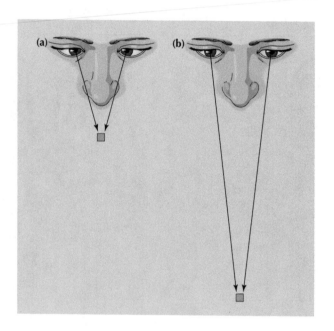

FIGURE 3.19

46

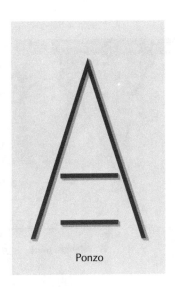

Ponzo

FIGURE 3.21

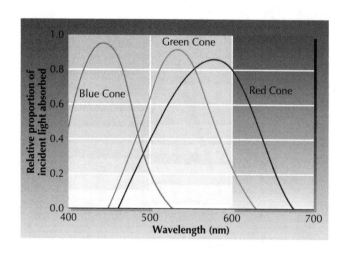

FIGURE 3.22

48

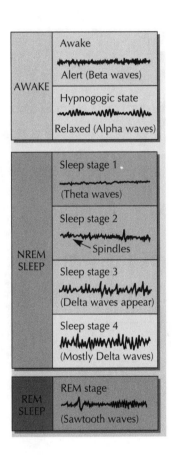

FIGURE 4.2

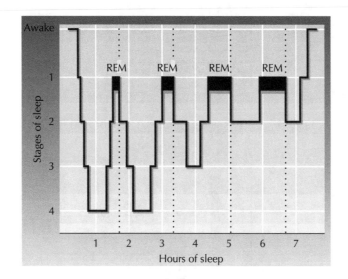

FIGURE 4.3   50

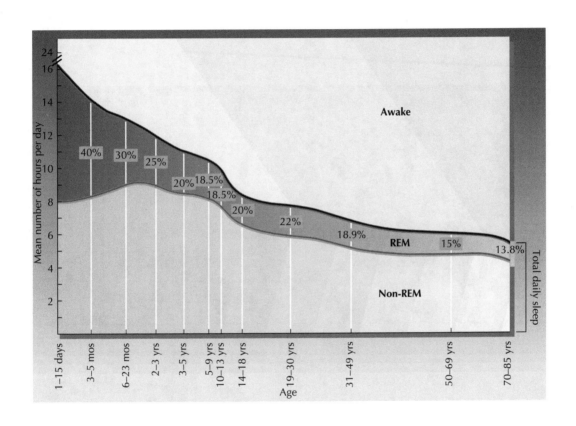

51

FIGURE 4.4

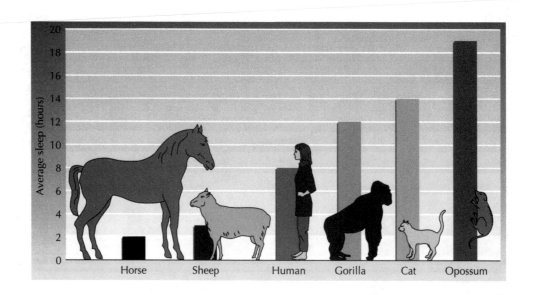

FIGURE 4.5 52

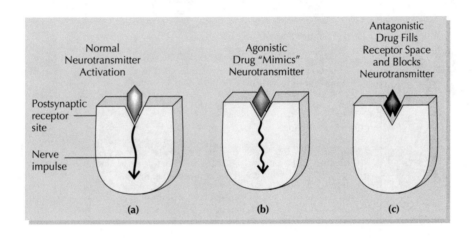

FIGURE 4.6

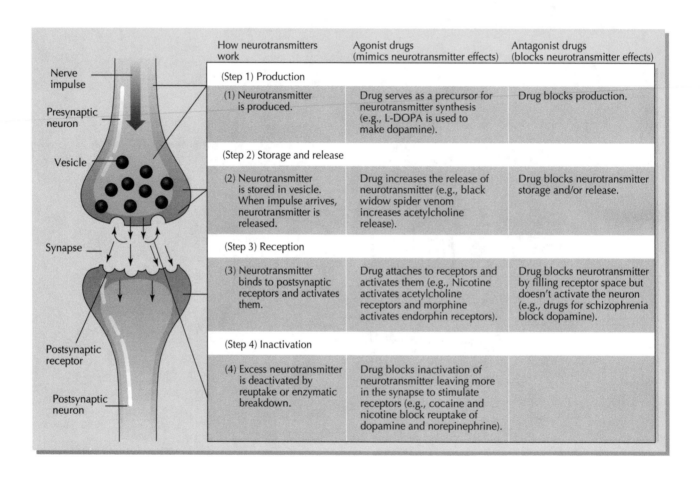

	How neurotransmitters work	Agonist drugs (mimics neurotransmitter effects)	Antagonist drugs (blocks neurotransmitter effects)
(Step 1) Production			
	(1) Neurotransmitter is produced.	Drug serves as a precursor for neurotransmitter synthesis (e.g., L-DOPA is used to make dopamine).	Drug blocks production.
(Step 2) Storage and release			
	(2) Neurotransmitter is stored in vesicle. When impulse arrives, neurotransmitter is released.	Drug increases the release of neurotransmitter (e.g., black widow spider venom increases acetylcholine release).	Drug blocks neurotransmitter storage and/or release.
(Step 3) Reception			
	(3) Neurotransmitter binds to postsynaptic receptors and activates them.	Drug attaches to receptors and activates them (e.g., Nicotine activates acetylcholine receptors and morphine activates endorphin receptors).	Drug blocks neurotransmitter by filling receptor space but doesn't activate the neuron (e.g., drugs for schizophrenia block dopamine).
(Step 4) Inactivation			
	(4) Excess neurotransmitter is deactivated by reuptake or enzymatic breakdown.	Drug blocks inactivation of neurotransmitter leaving more in the synapse to stimulate receptors (e.g., cocaine and nicotine block reuptake of dopamine and norepinephrine).	

FIGURE 4.7

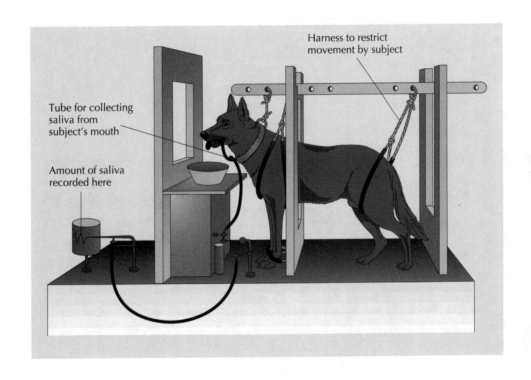

Harness to restrict
movement by subject

Tube for collecting
saliva from
subject's mouth

Amount of saliva
recorded here

FIGURE 5.1

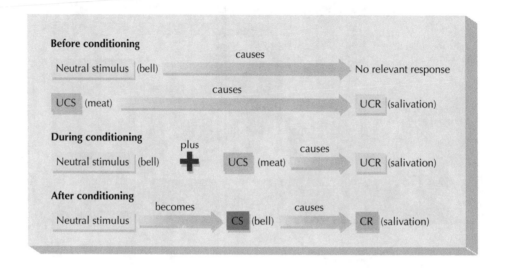

FIGURE 5.2   56

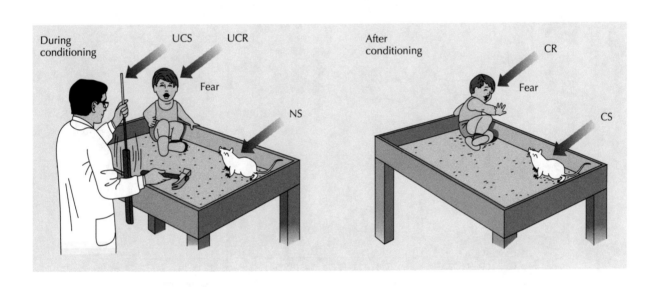

During
conditioning

UCS   UCR

Fear

NS

After
conditioning

CR

Fear

CS

FIGURE 5.3

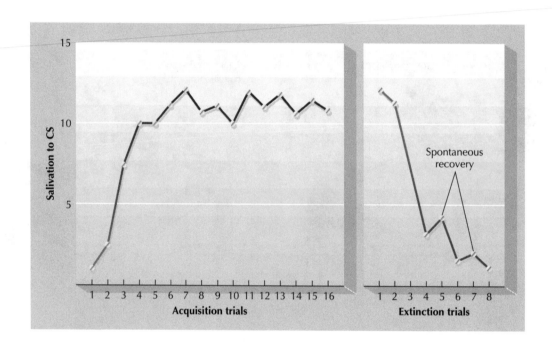

FIGURE 5.4

58

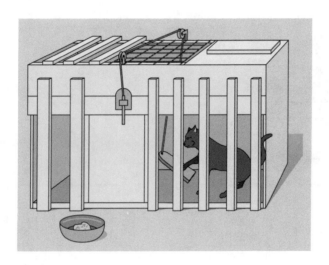

FIGURE 5.5

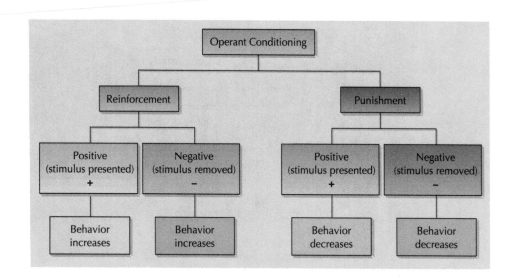

FIGURE 5.6

60

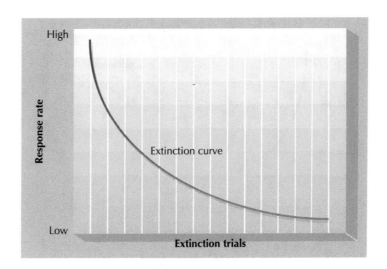

FIGURE 5.7

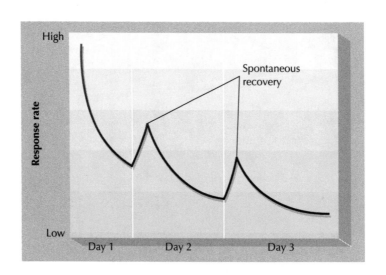

FIGURE 5.8   62

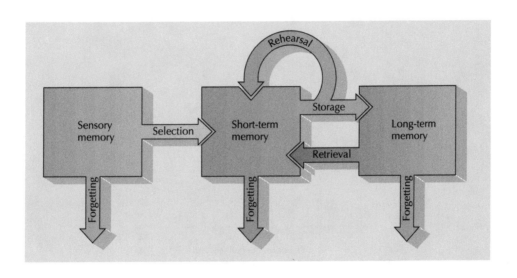

FIGURE 6.1

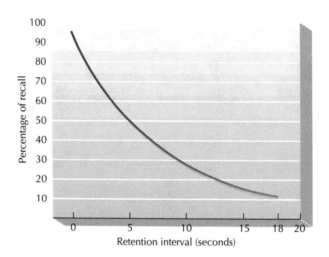

FIGURE 6.2   64

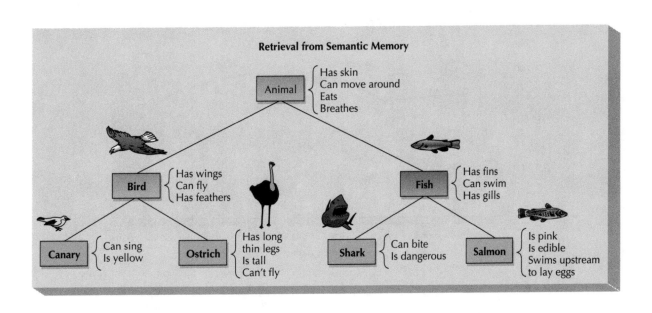

Retrieval from Semantic Memory

FIGURE 6.3

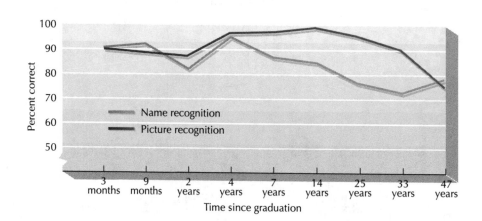

FIGURE 6.4   66

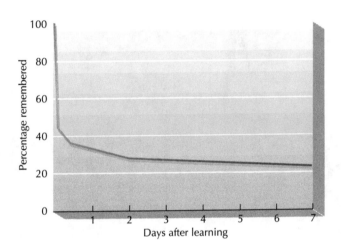

FIGURE 6.5

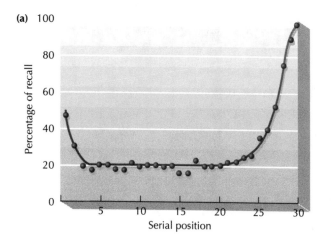

(a)

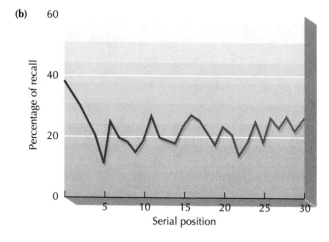

(b)

FIGURE 6.6

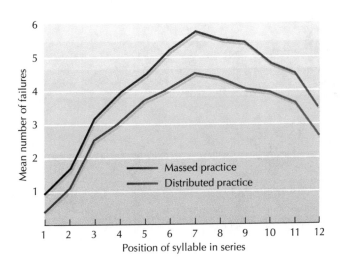

FIGURE 6.7

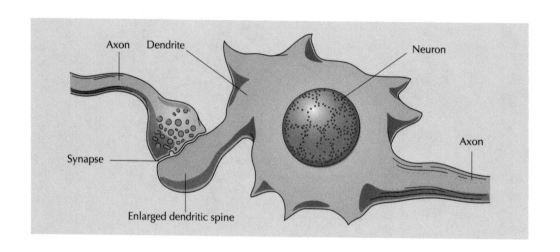

FIGURE 6.8   70

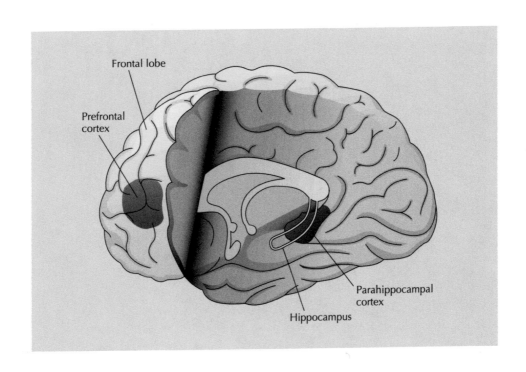

Frontal lobe

Prefrontal cortex

Parahippocampal cortex

Hippocampus

FIGURE 6.9

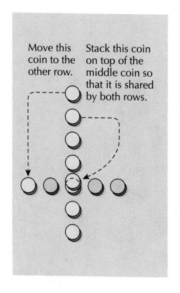

FIGURE 7.2   72

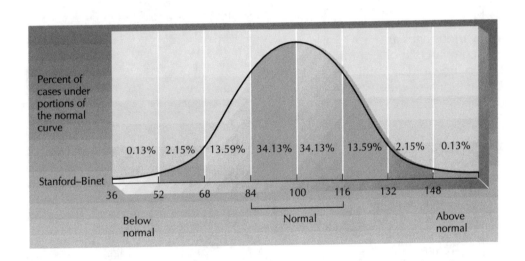

FIGURE 7.3

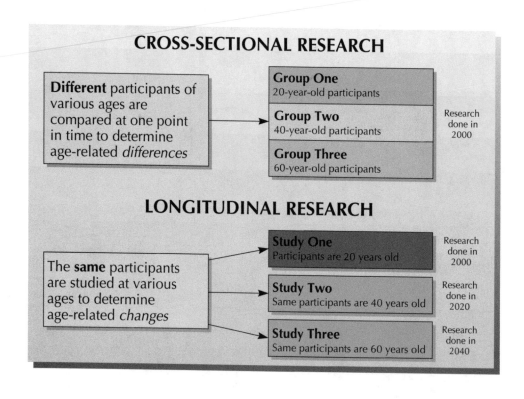

FIGURE 8.1

74

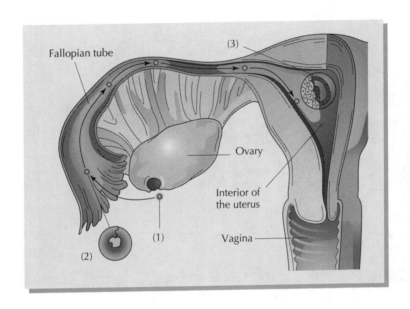

Fallopian tube

(3)

Ovary

Interior of
the uterus

(1)

Vagina

(2)

FIGURE 8.3a

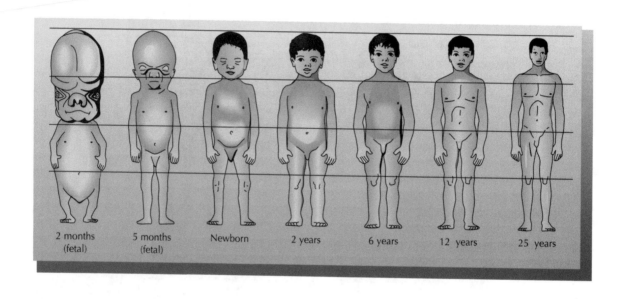

| 2 months (fetal) | 5 months (fetal) | Newborn | 2 years | 6 years | 12 years | 25 years |

FIGURE 8.5

76

Chin up
2.2 mo.

Rolls over
2.8 mo.

Sits with support
2.9 mo.

Sits alone
5.5 mo.

Stands holding furniture
5.8 mo.

Walks holding on
9.2 mo.

Stands alone
11.5 mo.

Walks alone
12.1 mo.

Walks up steps
17.1 mo.

FIGURE 8.6

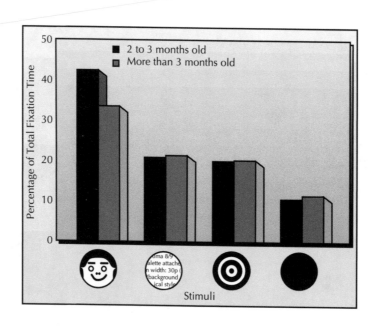

FIGURE 8.8

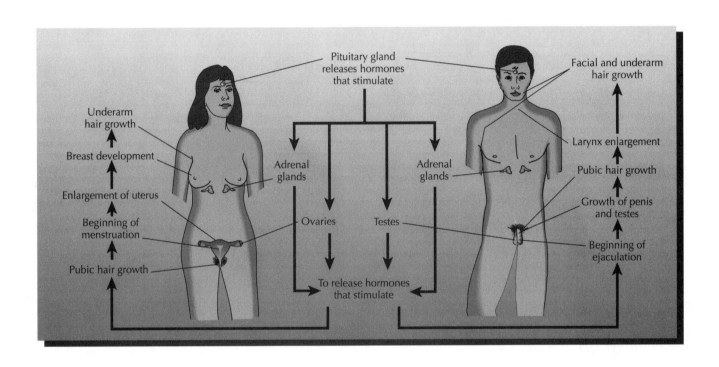

FIGURE 8.9

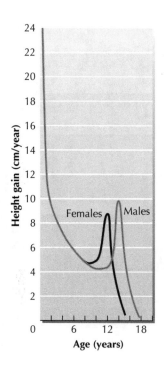

FIGURE 8.10   80

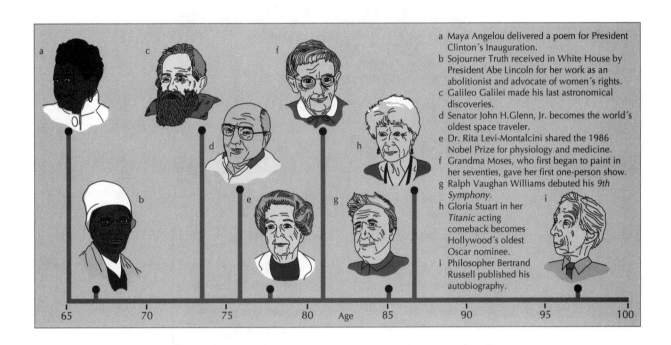

a Maya Angelou delivered a poem for President Clinton´s Inauguration.
b Sojourner Truth received in White House by President Abe Lincoln for her work as an abolitionist and advocate of women´s rights.
c Galileo Galilei made his last astronomical discoveries.
d Senator John H.Glenn, Jr. becomes the world´s oldest space traveler.
e Dr. Rita Levi-Montalcini shared the 1986 Nobel Prize for physiology and medicine.
f Grandma Moses, who first began to paint in her seventies, gave her first one-person show.
g Ralph Vaughan Williams debuted his *9th Symphony*.
h Gloria Stuart in her *Titanic* acting comeback becomes Hollywood´s oldest Oscar nominee.
i Philosopher Bertrand Russell published his autobiography.

Age

65   70   75   80   85   90   95   100

FIGURE 8.11

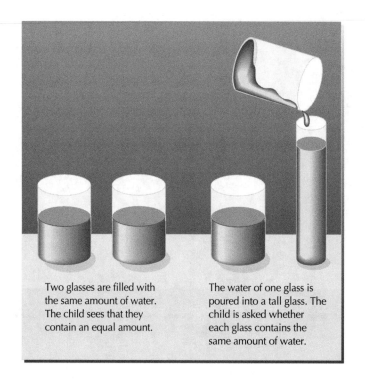

Two glasses are filled with the same amount of water. The child sees that they contain an equal amount.

The water of one glass is poured into a tall glass. The child is asked whether each glass contains the same amount of water.

FIGURE 8.14

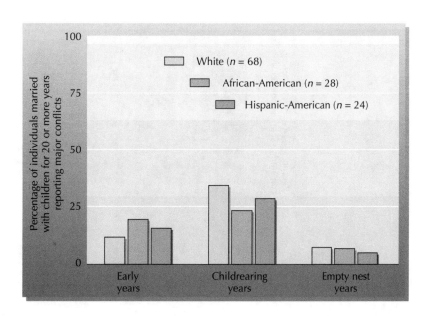

FIGURE 9.1

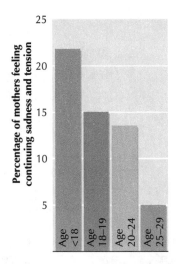

Mother's age at
birth of first offspring

FIGURE 9.2   84

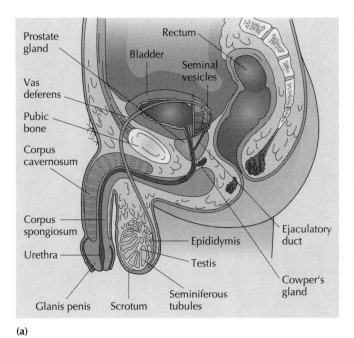

(a)

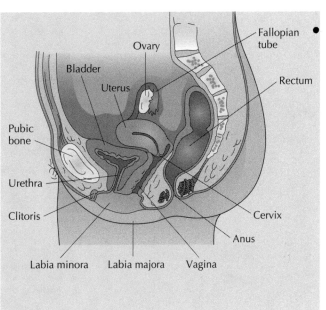

(b)

FIGURE 10.1

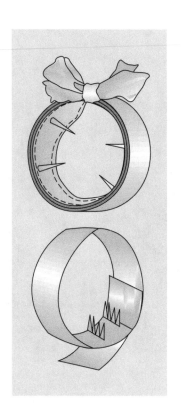

FIGURE 10.2   86

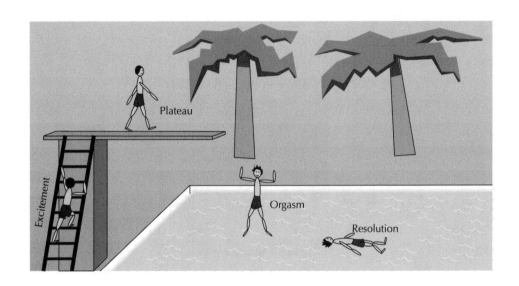

FIGURE 10.3

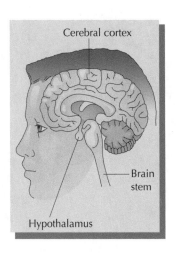

Cerebral cortex

Brain stem

Hypothalamus

FIGURE 10.4

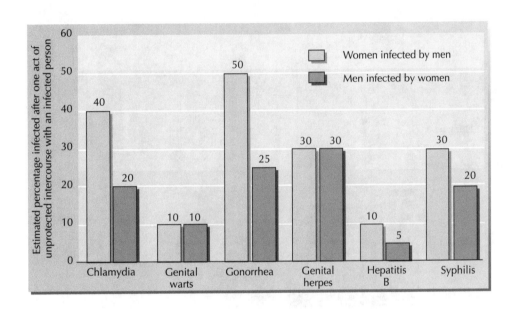

FIGURE 10.6

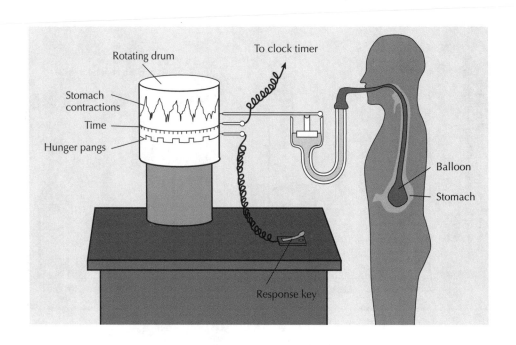

Rotating drum

Stomach
contractions

Time

Hunger pangs

To clock timer

Response key

Balloon

Stomach

FIGURE 11.1

90

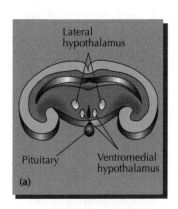

FIGURE 11.2a

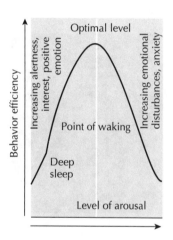

FIGURE 11.4

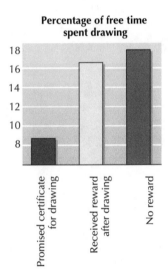

Percentage of free time spent drawing

(a)

- Promised certificate for drawing
- Received reward after drawing
- No reward

FIGURE 11.6a

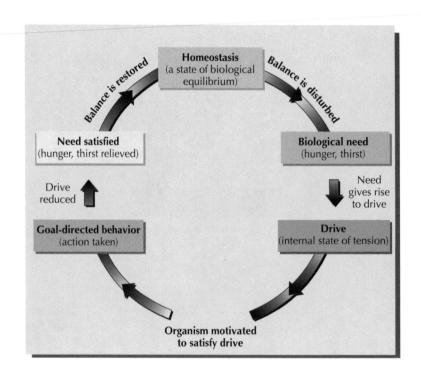

FIGURE 11.7

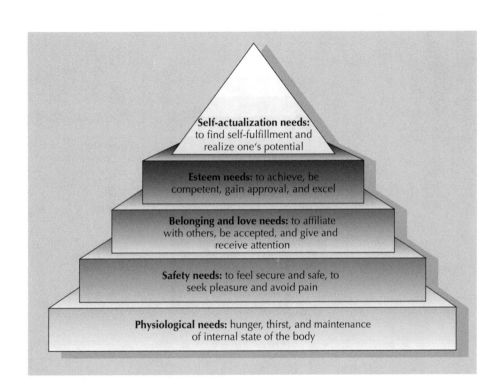

Self-actualization needs: to find self-fulfillment and realize one's potential

Esteem needs: to achieve, be competent, gain approval, and excel

Belonging and love needs: to affiliate with others, be accepted, and give and receive attention

Safety needs: to feel secure and safe, to seek pleasure and avoid pain

Physiological needs: hunger, thirst, and maintenance of internal state of the body

FIGURE 11.8

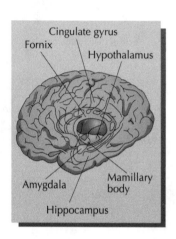

Cingulate gyrus

Fornix

Hypothalamus

Amygdala

Mamillary body

Hippocampus

FIGURE 11.9

96

Sympathetic		Parasympathetic
Pupils dilated	**Eyes**	Pupils constricted
Dry	**Mouth**	Salivating
Goose bumps, perspiration	**Skin**	No goose bumps
Respiration increased	**Lungs**	Respiration normal
Increased rate	**Heart**	Decreased rate
Increased epinephrine and norepinephrine	**Adrenal glands**	Decreased epinephrine and norepinephrine
Decreased motility	**Digestion**	Increased motility

FIGURE 11.10

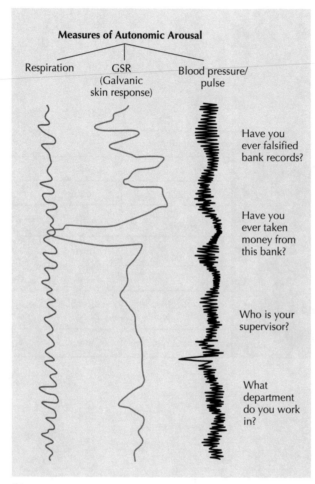

(b)

FIGURE 11.11b

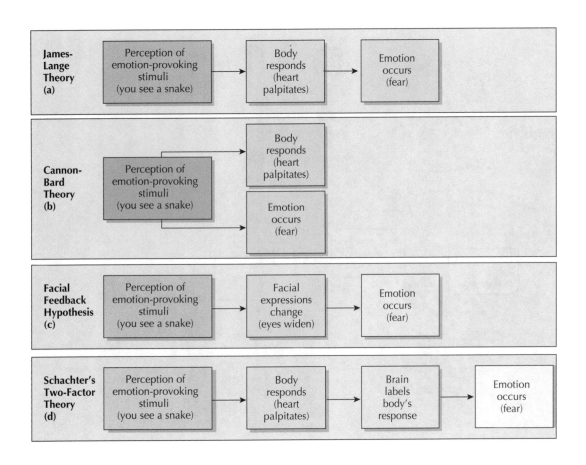

FIGURE 11.14

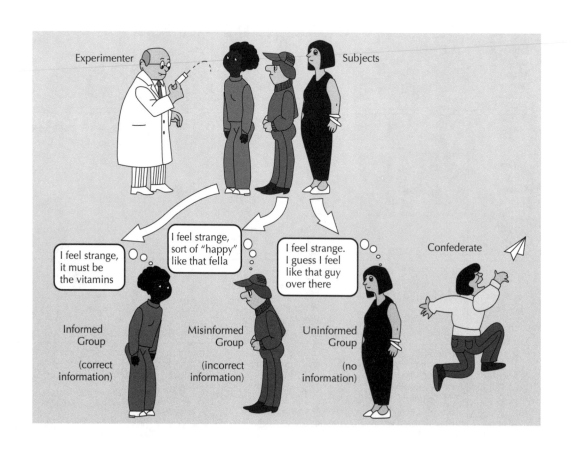

FIGURE 11.15

100

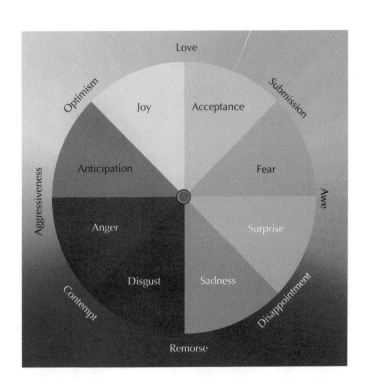

101

FIGURE 11.16

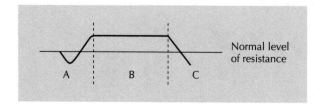

FIGURE 12.1   102

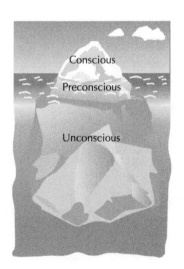

FIGURE 13.4

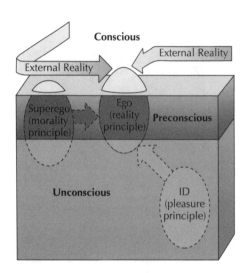

FIGURE 13.5

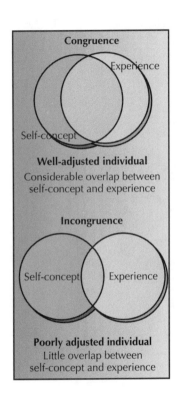

FIGURE 13.7

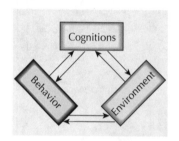

FIGURE 13.8

106

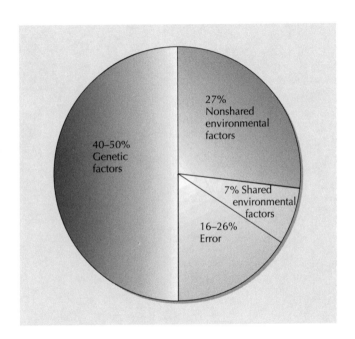

FIGURE 13.9

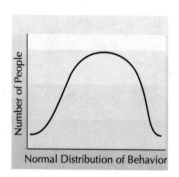

FIGURE 14.1   108

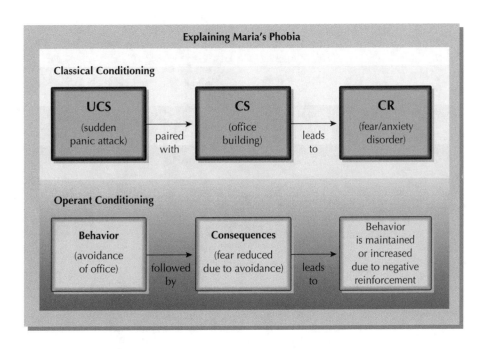

Explaining Maria's Phobia

Classical Conditioning

| UCS (sudden panic attack) | paired with | CS (office building) | leads to | CR (fear/anxiety disorder) |

Operant Conditioning

| Behavior (avoidance of office) | followed by | Consequences (fear reduced due to avoidance) | leads to | Behavior is maintained or increased due to negative reinforcement |

FIGURE 14.2

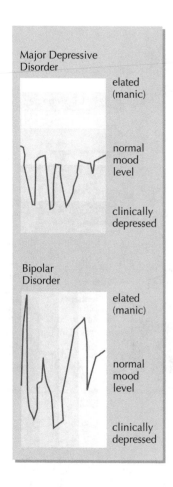

FIGURE 14.3   110

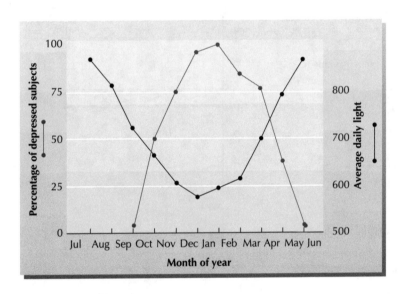

FIGURE 14.4

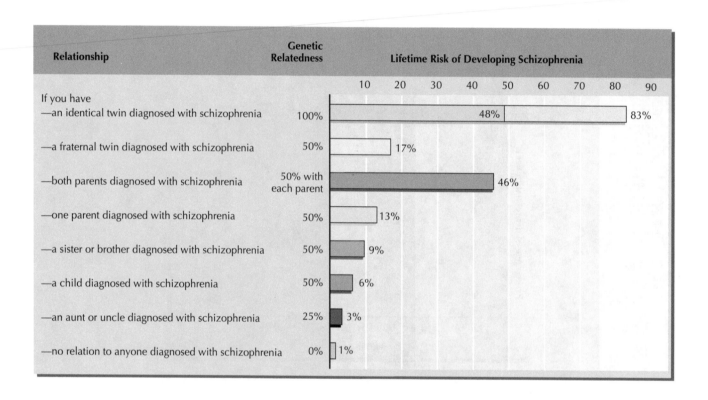

Relationship	Genetic Relatedness	Lifetime Risk of Developing Schizophrenia

If you have
—an identical twin diagnosed with schizophrenia — 100% — 48% / 83%

—a fraternal twin diagnosed with schizophrenia — 50% — 17%

—both parents diagnosed with schizophrenia — 50% with each parent — 46%

—one parent diagnosed with schizophrenia — 50% — 13%

—a sister or brother diagnosed with schizophrenia — 50% — 9%

—a child diagnosed with schizophrenia — 50% — 6%

—an aunt or uncle diagnosed with schizophrenia — 25% — 3%

—no relation to anyone diagnosed with schizophrenia — 0% — 1%

FIGURE 14.5

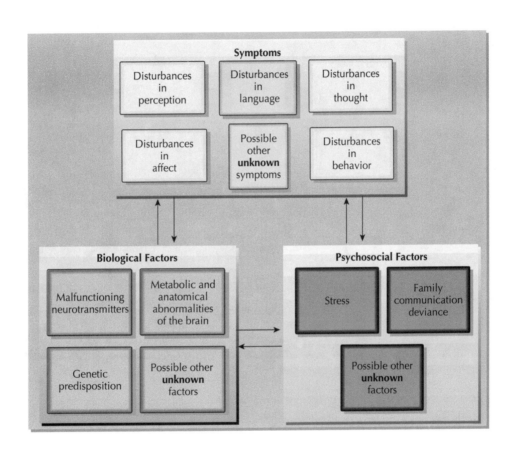

FIGURE 14.7

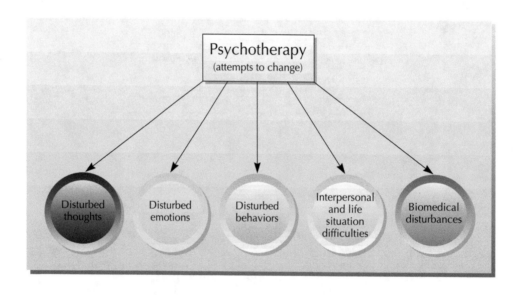

FIGURE 15.1

114

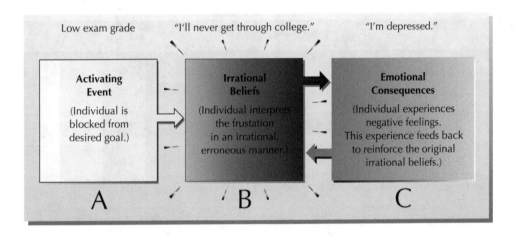

Low exam grade   "I'll never get through college."   "I'm depressed."

Activating Event

(Individual is blocked from desired goal.)

A

Irrational Beliefs

(Individual interprets the frustation in an irrational, erroneous manner.)

B

Emotional Consequences

(Individual experiences negative feelings. This experience feeds back to reinforce the original irrational beliefs.)

C

FIGURE 15.3

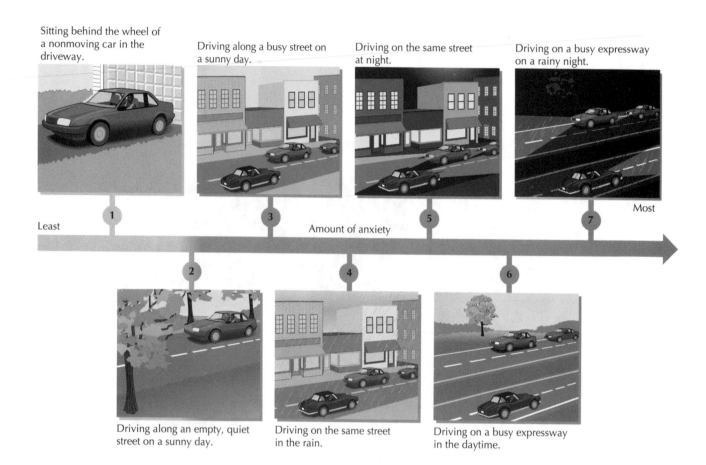

Sitting behind the wheel of a nonmoving car in the driveway.

Driving along a busy street on a sunny day.

Driving on the same street at night.

Driving on a busy expressway on a rainy night.

Least

Amount of anxiety

Most

Driving along an empty, quiet street on a sunny day.

Driving on the same street in the rain.

Driving on a busy expressway in the daytime.

FIGURE 15.4

116

UCS
(drug in alcohol)

UCR
(nausea)

CS
(alcohol)

CR
(nausea)

FIGURE 15.5

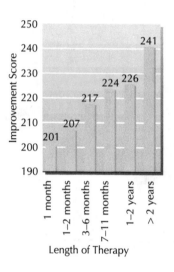

FIGURE 15.7   118

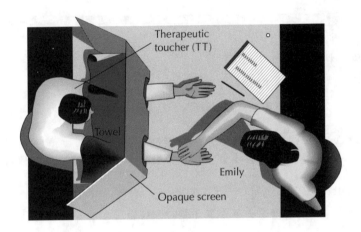

FIGURE 15.8

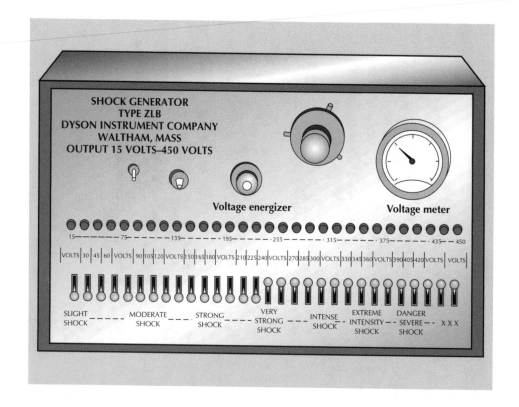

FIGURE 16.1

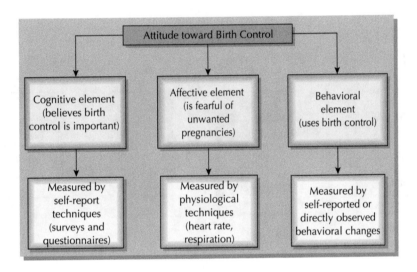

FIGURE 16.2

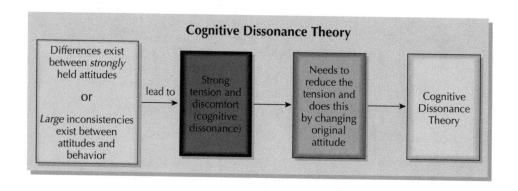

FIGURE 16.3   122

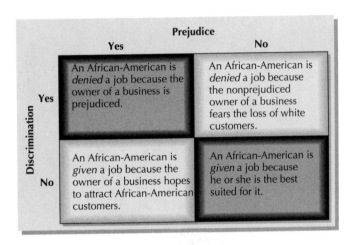

FIGURE 16.4

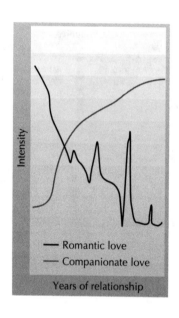

Intensity

Romantic love
Companionate love

Years of relationship

FIGURE 16.6

124

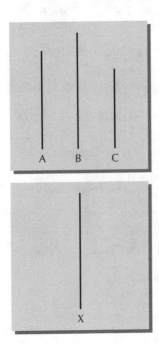

FIGURE 16.7

Antecedent Conditions

1 A highly cohesive group of decision makers
2 Insulation of the group from outside influences
3 A directive leader
4 Lack of procedures to ensure careful consideration of the pros and cons of alternative actions
5 High stress from external threats with little hope of finding a better solution than that favored by the leader

Strong desire for group consensus—The groupthink tendency

Symptoms of Groupthink

1 Illusion of invulnerability
2 Belief in the morality of the group
3 Collective rationalizations
4 Stereotypes of outgroups
5 Self-censorship of doubts and dissenting opinions
6 Illusion of unanimity
7 Direct pressure on dissenters

Symptoms of Poor Decision Making

1 An incomplete survey of alternative courses of action
2 An incomplete survey of group objectives
3 Failure to examine risks of the preferred choice
4 Failure to reappraise rejected alternatives
5 Poor search for relevant information
6 Selective bias in processing information
7 Failure to develop contingency plans

Low probability of successful outcome

FIGURE 16.8

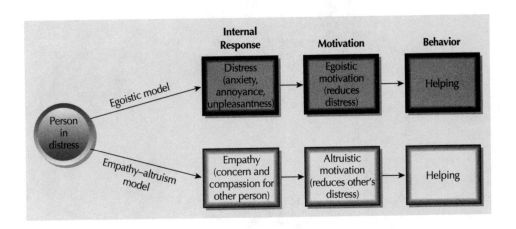

FIGURE 16.9

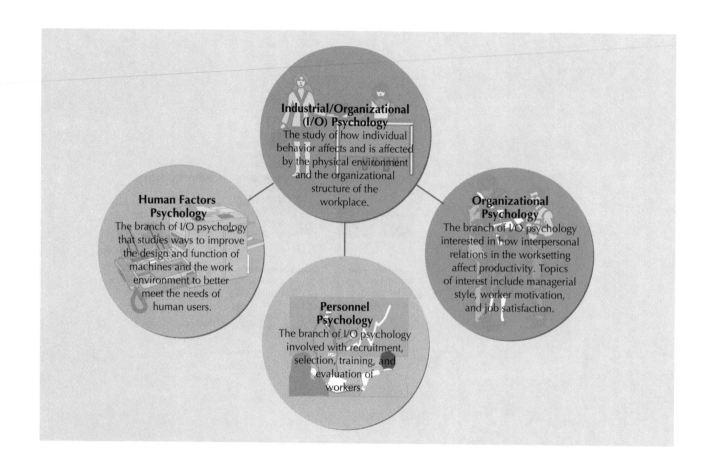

FIGURE 17.1

128

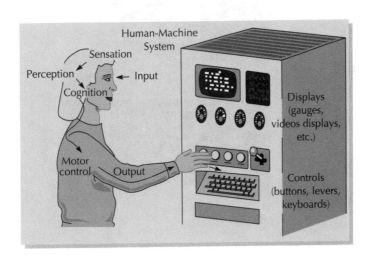

FIGURE 17.2

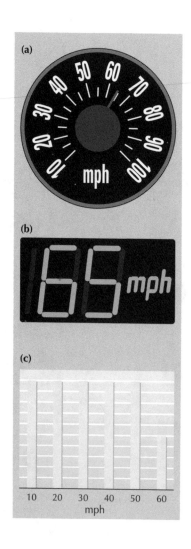

FIGURE 17.3

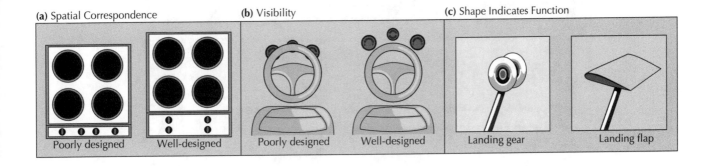

(a) Spatial Correspondence

Poorly designed — Well-designed

(b) Visibility

Poorly designed — Well-designed

(c) Shape Indicates Function

Landing gear — Landing flap

FIGURE 17.4

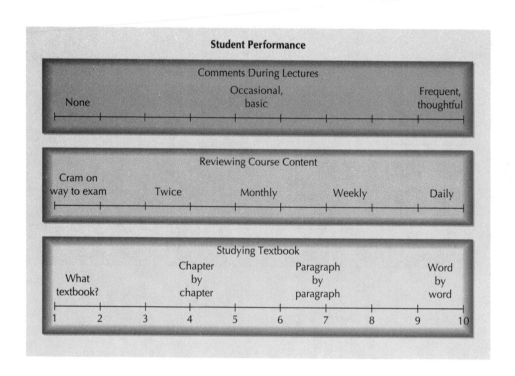

FIGURE 17.5

132

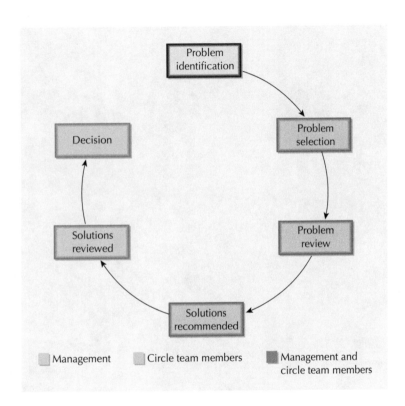

FIGURE 17.6